Saint Angela Merici

Leading people to God

Written by Sr. Maryellen Keefe, OSU

Illustrated by Augusta Curreli

Edited and adapted by Mary Cabrini Durkin, OSU
and Patricia Edward Jablonski, FSP

BOOKS & MEDIA
BOSTON

English edition copyright © 2000, Daughters of St. Paul

ISBN: 0-8198-7031-5

*Layout :*Éditions du signe

© 2000, Éditions du Signe, 1 rue Alfred Kastler, B.P. 94 - F 67038 Strasbourg

Printed in France by PPO, Pantin

Other titles in this series:

Saint Anthony of Padua
Proclaimer of the Good News

Saint Catherine Labouré
Mary's messenger

Saint Colette
In the footsteps of Saint Francis and Saint Clare

Saint Francis of Assisi
God's gentle knight

Saint John Bosco
The friend of children and young people

Saint Thérèse of Lisieux
And the "little way" of love

Saint Vincent de Paul
Servant of charity

Do you ever wonder how to find God?

This is the story of Saint Angela Merici. Even when she was a young girl, she knew that God was leading her with love. She wanted to stay close to God. Angela listened to God in her own heart. She learned to see God in the people and the world around her.

Angela led other people to find God in their hearts and lives, too.

This little book will tell you about her adventures and about how she helped people. Before you read it, turn to the back of the book. There you will find an explanation of some words which may be new to you.

Would you like to have Angela as your friend in heaven? She will show you that God is always with you.

In the little lakeside town of Desenzano in northern Italy, stands a huge castle that overlooks the surrounding valley.

On Via Castello, the main road running down to Lake Garda, there are several houses and shops. In #96 lived the Merici family.

The family was very happy: a baby girl was born to John and Catherine Merici in the year 1474. She was named Angela. There were four Merici children altogether — two boys and two girls.

Their father used to gather the family around the fire each evening for story hour. Sometimes he would read from the Bible. Sometimes he would let the children take turns choosing a favorite saint's life.

"It's my turn tonight, Papa," said Angela. "Read us the story of Saint Ursula."

"She was so brave!" added her sister.

In this way, young Angela learned about many heroes and martyrs who had generously served God. She wanted to be just like them some day, giving her life for the love of Jesus.

Angela was especially close to her sister Gianna Maria. Whenever they played games by the lake, the two of them would try to lose their brothers so that they could talk all by themselves. At other times, all four would have a wild game of tag.

While Angela was still small, her parents bought some farmland a few miles from Lake Garda.
"The place is called Le Grezze, which means The Sheepfold," Mr. Merici told his children, "and we're going to have a cow and three goats."

Soon enough their grapevines were full of grapes and there were many olives growing on the olive trees. The children helped their mother to milk the animals and led them to the fields for grazing.

They enjoyed being out in the fresh air and sunshine, but sometimes they got hungry. "Let's have some yummy figs," Gianna Maria would say. They didn't realize that they were on their neighbor's property. Their father would have to pay a fine for such "law-breaking" whenever they got caught!

In the evenings when he wasn't too tired, Mr. Merici would teach his children to read. He wanted them to learn as much as they could, since there was no chance for them to go to school. "Papa, let me read tonight," Angela would insist with delight. And often she would read by herself the stories she had already learned by heart.

But before long, something very sad happened. In just a short time, both of Angela's parents died. Then, Gianna Maria became very, very ill. In a few days, she also died. Angela had never felt so sad. Even worse, she was afraid that her dear sister might not be in heaven. Angela prayed that God would let her know.

Meanwhile, there was a lot of work to be done. Every day, besides her own chores, Angela now did her sister's jobs too. After doing laundry, cleaning the house, and baking bread, Angela would pack lunches for the seven workers who helped on the farm. She would carry the lunches out to the field. Many times she ate her own under a shady tree.

One day in a place called Brudazzo, Angela was with some workers who were singing and picking olives to be pressed for oil. All of a sudden she saw what appeared to be angels going up and down a ladder that looked as if it reached as high as heaven. With them—could it be?—was her sister—just bursting with joy! "I'm in heaven, Angela!" she seemed to say. Yes, Gianna Maria was really in heaven. Angela was very happy and relieved.

But there was more. Her sister had a message: "Angela, one day you will gather a group of young women like me. You will form them into a community called a Company. They will have a special work to do in the Church." As the vision disappeared, Angela knelt down and thanked Jesus for her sister's happiness. She wondered what the message could mean. She wouldn't understand until many years later.

Now, sixteen years old and an orphan, Angela had to move with her younger brother to the nearby lakeside town of Salò, where their Uncle and Aunt Biancosi welcomed them. The Merici children had often enjoyed holidays and family celebrations there. Bartholomew, their cousin, was especially glad to have his cousins moving in, because he was an only child. But for Angela this new home would mean a very different kind of life.

The town of Salò was bigger than Desenzano. The people there had many parties and celebrations for every season and feast. Angela, with her beautiful blond hair, had many admirers. But her beauty didn't make her proud. She kept thinking, instead, about God — the Lord of Beauty and Truth.

Although everyone was eager to have her meet some good young man, Angela was in love with God. Her deep relationship with him was already changing her life. She was friendly to everyone and appreciated all the efforts her aunt and uncle made to help her adjust to her new life. But what she really wanted was more time to spend alone praying.

Angela helped with the housework. She had friendly talks with the people she met as she drew water from the fountain or well. Yet at the same time, something else was happening. More and more Angela began to notice God's presence in her life. More and more she wished she had a quieter spot where she could listen to and speak with him in her heart.

In her free time Angela would read her father's book on the lives of the saints. Teaching her to read had been one of her father's most precious gifts to her. From the time she was little, the saints' lives had inspired Angela. She wanted to live as they had lived.

When she was eighteen, following the inspiration of the Holy Spirit, Angela spoke with a Franciscan priest at her parish. Before long, she decided, "I want to become a member of the Franciscan Third Order."

In this way she would be able to receive Holy Communion more often. As a member she would be called Sister Angela. She would wear the simple robe of the Franciscans and a white veil. She would no longer go to dances or fancy parties.

She would fast before holy days and during Advent and Lent. She would pray the morning and evening prayer of the Church in her parish, and become a peacemaker among her relatives, friends, and the townspeople. She would attend Mass every day and a priest would give her good advice on how to follow Jesus more closely. She would eat vegetables, fruit, and fish, and sleep on a mat instead of in a luxurious bed.

Angela moved back to Le Grezze, which was now her brother's home. There she was welcomed by her sister-in-law. In the evenings, their children would beg, "Aunt Angela, tell us stories of your favorite saints." Angela was always happy to share with them what she had learned when she was little. At the end of a story, she would smile and say, "And that's how your Grandfather Merici told it to me."

Angela attended Mass early each morning. Then she joined the workers in the fields. She also visited the sick and took care of poor neighbors. Sometimes she brought them food. At other times she explained how they could follow Jesus and live the Gospel better. The people respected her as Sister Angela and were happy that she had come home. They realized they had a special person living among them.

Sometimes Angela would sail to Salò to see the priest who gave her good advice and to visit her aunt and uncle. Then, one day in the summer of 1516, the priest asked her if she could go to the city of Brescia for a while to comfort her friend, Catherine Patengola. Catherine's husband and children had just died in a war. Brescia was getting over one of its many wars with its neighboring cities.

Catherine had no one left except a little grandaughter, Isabella. Angela was happy to help her friend in any way she could. Besides doing housework, she would read the Bible with Catherine and help her to pray. She also got to know Catherine's nephew, Giralomo, and his friend Anthony Romano. After a while, she moved into an apartment in Anthony's home, where she lived for about fourteen years.

During these years Angela made friends with good men and women who were helping poor and sick people in Brescia. They started a hospice for homeless people who were dying. Some of the women took care of orphans and taught them. Everyone depended on Angela for wise advice. Her love for Jesus was catching! She helped many people grow closer to him.

Then, in 1524, Anthony invited Angela and her cousin Bartholomew to go with him on a pilgrimage to the Holy Land. A pilgrimage is a special trip made to a holy place. People go on a pilgrimage for different reasons. Many want to honor the saints and visit the holy places. Others want to make up for sinful things they've done. Some, like Angela, desire to be in the places where Jesus lived and died.

First Angela and Bartholomew had to travel on horseback to Venice.

There they dressed in pilgrims' clothing--a cloak, a large brimmed hat tied under the chin, and a backpack worn over the shoulder. Each person took along a walking staff and a water bottle.

The pilgrims walked together in procession down to the ship. Before boarding they received a blessing to protect them from dangerous storms and pirate attacks.

Along the way, when their ship docked at the island of Crete, something unexpected happened. Angela's eyes became infected and she couldn't see! So her two companions had to guide her.

They led her to all the holy places as you would lead a blind person. Even though she couldn't see with her eyes, Angela's heart saw more deeply into the mystery of Jesus' suffering as she followed the road to the place of his crucifixion and death. It's easy to imagine her love and great respect as she knelt to kiss the place where Jesus' cross once stood.

On the way home, Angela's group set sail for Cyprus, where their ship took on cargo. Next it stopped at Candia. There, to everyone's great surprise, Angela was suddenly able to see again as she prayed before a crucifix.

On October 4, the feast of Saint Francis, the group of pilgrims was joined by the Duke of Candia for the last part of the journey to Venice. Almost right away a fierce storm began. For nine days angry winds, lightning, and thunder continued. Two other ships sank, but the pilgrims were only blown off course. Landing at Tunisia on the northern coast of Africa, they were sure that Angela's prayers had brought them to safety. They thanked God that they were still alive.

But soon they ran into another danger — a fleet of Turkish pirates! Guns were fired and the pirate captain came aboard to speak to the Duke. Then the pirates sailed away. But secretly, they waited nearby to attack and take prisoners. The pilgrims were able to escape, and everyone believed that Angela's prayers had helped them again.

When they finally returned to Venice, Angela and her two friends stayed there for several weeks. Pilgrims like them often gave weeks of service to others as a way of showing gratitude for the hospitality they had received. While she was in Venice, Angela welcomed many visitors. They wanted to meet this holy woman. They said, "We know it was your prayers that saved us from the pirates."

Nearby was a hospital. "Sister Angela," some important people of Venice begged, "stay here and help us run this hospital."

But, knowing that God wanted her to start organizing a Company of friends and followers in Brescia, she left quickly. She traveled back home in a closed carriage since it was almost winter. She arrived in Brescia on November 25, the feast of Saint Catherine of Alexandria, a virgin-martyr whom Angela admired very much.

In 1525, which the Pope had declared to be a Jubilee year, the city of Rome was fighting both its enemies and the plague. Angela wasn't afraid of these dangers. She decided to make a pilgrimage to Rome. She wanted to receive the special blessings of the Jubilee year given to pilgrims who visited and prayed at the four major basilicas. She wanted to honor the relics of the martyrs and visit their graves down in the catacombs.

During the two weeks that she spent in Rome, she had a personal visit with the Pope. But when the Pope asked her, "Would you consider staying in Rome to be director of an orphanage?" Angela humbly excused herself. She happily went back to Brescia, because she knew that she had to form her Company soon.

One time, two men in Brescia had challenged each other to a duel. They were planning to fight with swords until one or both of them died.

Their wives went to Angela, "Sister Angela, please help us!" they begged. "You must get our husbands to stop fighting!"

So Angela went and spoke with each of the men. How brave she was! Finally, they agreed to end the argument. The whole city was amazed.

Another time she obtained a pardon for a servant of Louis Gonzaga, a harsh nobleman. The servant was being very severely punished for something wrong he had done. Angela made a special trip to see Louis and try to persuade him to be merciful. Her words, inspired by the Holy Spirit, convinced Louis to forgive the man and release him from the punishment. Angela wasn't afraid to go on this difficult mission. And once again, she succeeded.

But Angela was best at helping other women. They would talk to her about their problems. And she would give them wise advice. In this way she helped bring love and peace to husbands and wives, children and parents, brothers, sisters, and cousins.

As they talked of the problems facing younger girls, many women urged Angela to do something. "The young women of Brescia are suffering from the dangers that come with living in the middle of violence. Sister Angela, we must do something to help them!"

Angela welcomed all the women who came to her, the poor as well as the rich. Her gentle words gave them so much light.
"Sister Angela, my girl is only interested in clothes and parties.…"
"Be patient! Tell her Jesus wants to be her best friend."

Brescia expected to be invaded in another war in 1529. Angela and many other people had to escape for a while to the nearby town of Cremona. While they were there, her friend Augustine Gallo was impressed by Angela's kindness toward the amazing number of people who came to visit her from morning till night. Men and women of all ages, members of the court, and even the Duke of Milan, came to Angela for advice and a word of comfort. The result was that many people began to live in ways more pleasing to God.

When it was peaceful in Brescia again, the refugees went home. Angela accepted an invitation to live with the Gallo family for a while. Then, needing a space to welcome the many people who were coming to her for help, she moved to an apartment near the public fountain, next to Saint Afra's Church.

Now she was ready to begin the project Gianna Maria had told her about in the vision. She was ready to found her Company. Its members would help her to care for young girls in Brescia.

She would give this Company the name of Saint Ursula, a martyr whose courageous death for her faith in Jesus had inspired many people. In Venice Angela had seen several large paintings of Saint Ursula and her companions.

She decided they would be good role models for her Company of young women. They would need the strength of the martyrs' faith as they dedicated themselves completely to Jesus, while continuing to live among the people.

Like Angela, the members of the Company chose not to marry because they gave their hearts to Jesus. They would try to live according to the Gospel, as Jesus taught his first followers. They would especially try to love everyone.

Together with Angela they would help young girls to escape the dangers of the streets. With the Company to guide and protect them, many of these girls would learn to believe in themselves. They would begin to lead good lives and find useful work to do.

Because these women would be the start of something new in the Church, they would need a new Rule of life. Angela dictated the Rule to her lawyer friend Gabriel Cozzano. He wrote it down for her.

"Mother Angela, when will your Company officially begin?" Gabriel asked.

"On the Feast of St. Catherine, who is one of my favorite saints!"

On the feast of Saint Catherine, November 25, 1535, twenty-eight women joined to begin the Company of Saint Ursula. After attending Mass together, each one wrote her name in the Book of the Company. This was their promise to live according to the new Rule. The members were called Ursulines. After only four years there were 150 of them!

They would meet with Angela in her apartment to pray together and share ideas about how to help each other in the life they were leading for God. By their good example, they were an inspiration to other families in Brescia. And soon enough they would help even the Church. Most of the Ursulines had jobs. When they came together for meetings, Angela gave them time to talk about their everyday lives, to pray and to learn. She made sure that they had fun together. They dressed simply, attended daily Mass, and prayed afterward at home.

Angela trained some of these women as leaders. The leaders would visit each Ursuline at home. They would give her good advice about trying to live like Jesus and would make sure she was all right.

Angela was getting old and weaker. She became very ill. She spent her last days dictating to her friend Gabriel the holy thoughts and instructions that she wanted to leave the women in charge of the Company.

She urged them to live in love, united with one heart and will, and to be faithful. She told them, "You must be like loving mothers, caring for your spiritual daughters and teaching them with devotion."

She promised them, "God will help you. And I will always be your faithful friend in heaven."

Angela's last words were, "Now I am leaving you. Be consoled and have a lively faith and hope. But first, I want you to be blessed in the name of the Father, and of the Son, and of the Holy Spirit. Amen."
At 3:30 P.M. on Tuesday, January 27, 1540, Angela died.

Dressed in her brown robe, her body was carried to the Church of Saint Afra. For three nights a brilliant star shone over the church. Her body remained in the church for thirty days, but without any sign of decay. In fact, her skin stayed soft. An artist came to paint her. His painting shows her in the peaceful sleep of death. Her face seems to glow with holiness.

Today her body lies in a beautiful glass case above an altar in Saint Afra's Church--now known as the Shrine of Saint Angela Merici.

After Angela's death, the Company of Saint Ursula grew and spread, first throughout Italy, then to every continent. Ursulines have brought the Gospel all over the world. Some of Angela's followers became known as the Order of Saint Ursula.

Today Ursulines serve in schools, parishes, colleges, hospitals, prisons, and many other places where people need their help. They try to live as Angela did—trusting in God who loves them and looking for ways to serve others.

Ready to share their talents and their love, they rely on Jesus and remember Angela's promise: "I will always be with you, helping your prayer and your work."

A few words to help you better understand St. Angela's life...

Basilica
A large church built in a special design.

Catacombs
Underground tunnels and rooms, especially in Rome, where early martyrs were buried, and where Mass was celebrated.

Company
A group of people who share their lives as they work for the Gospel.

Fasting
Eating less than usual for a spiritual reason.

Fleet
A group of ships sailing together.

Duke
The ruler of an area within a country.

Hospice
A special place where dying people are cared for.

Holy Land
Where the events of the Bible took place.

Jubilee
A year of special prayer, celebration, and pilgrimages, especially to Rome.

Martyr
A person who remains strong in the Christian faith, even though he or she is killed for it.

Plague
A terrible disease that is very contagious.

Relic
A piece of bone or cloth which is treated with respect because it belonged to a saint.

Rule
Guidelines for a particular religious way of life.

Prayer

*Saint Angela,
as I begin a new day,
help me to act as you did
while you were here on earth.
Help me to pray as you did,
thanking God for his many gifts.
I want to be ready to share what I have
with those who have less than I do.*

*When following Jesus isn't easy,
remind me to go to him for help.
Teach me to join any pain, or loneliness,
or frustration I have
with Jesus' suffering on the cross.
Help me to forgive the people who hurt me
and to ask God's blessing on them.
Most of all, help me to use my talents
to make the world a better place, as you did,
Saint Angela.*

Amen.

BOOKS & MEDIA

The Daughters of St. Paul operate book and media centers at the following addresses. Visit, call or write the one nearest you today, or find us on the World Wide Web, www.pauline.org

CALIFORNIA
    3908 Sepulveda Blvd., Culver City, CA 90230; 310-397-8676
    5945 Balboa Ave., San Diego, CA 92111; 619-565-9181
    46 Geary Street, San Francisco, CA 94108; 415-781-5180

FLORIDA
    145 S.W. 107th Ave., Miami, FL 33174; 305-559-6715

HAWAII
    1143 Bishop Street, Honolulu, HI 96813; 808-521-2731

ILLINOIS
    172 North Michigan Ave., Chicago, IL 60601; 312-346-4228

LOUISIANA
    4403 Veterans Memorial Blvd., Metairie, LA 70006; 504-887-7631

MASSACHUSETTS
    50 St. Paul's Ave., Jamaica Plain, Boston, MA 02130; 617-522-8911
    Rte. 1, 885 Providence Hwy., Dedham, MA 02026; 781-326-5385

MISSOURI
    9804 Watson Rd., St. Louis, MO 63126; 314-965-3512

NEW JERSEY
    561 U.S. Route 1, Wick Plaza, Edison, NJ 08817; 732-572-1200

NEW YORK
    150 East 52nd Street, New York, NY 10022; 212-754-1110
    78 Fort Place, Staten Island, NY 10301; 718-447-5071

OHIO
    2105 Ontario Street, Cleveland, OH 44115; 216-621-9427

PENNSYLVANIA
    9171-A Roosevelt Blvd., Philadelphia, PA 19114; 215-676-9494

SOUTH CAROLINA
    243 King Street, Charleston, SC 29401; 843-577-0175

TENNESSEE
    4811 Poplar Ave., Memphis, TN 38117; 901-761-2987

TEXAS
    114 Main Plaza, San Antonio, TX 78205; 210-224-8101

VIRGINIA
    1025 King Street, Alexandria, VA 22314; 703-549-3806

CANADA
    3022 Dufferin Street, Toronto, Ontario, Canada M6B 3T5; 416-781-9131
    1155 Yonge Street, Toronto, Ontario, Canada M4T 1W2; 416-934-3440